IMAGES OF LIBERTY

★　　★　　★　　★　　★

IMAGES OF LIBERTY

★   ★   ★   ★   ★   ★

By MICHAEL GRUMET

Arbor House
New York

10 9 8 7 6 5 4 3 2 1

Library of Congress Cataloging in Publication Data

Grumet, Michael.
    Images of Liberty.

    1. Statue of Liberty (New York, N.Y.) in art.
2. Statue of Liberty (New York, N.Y.) 3. Art,
Modern—20th century. I. Title.
N8251.S25G78   1986   704.9′4973′0924   86-1119
ISBN 0-87795-808-4
ISBN 0-87795-782-7 (pbk.)

Manufactured in the United States of America

*Frontispiece art: Human Statue of Liberty made up of 18,000 men, Camp Dodge, Des
Moines, Iowa, 1918.* Arthur Mole, photographer.

*Page 1 art: 1890 wood Statue of Liberty. The Edison Institute, Henry Ford Museum &
Greenfield Museum.*

DESIGN BY LAURA HOUGH

To Sally, also known as Sarah,
also known as Sarita, also known as Mom;
and to Ethel Camiel, my oldest friend.
A special thank-you to my agent, Malaga Baldi,
and my editor, Michael Carter.

CONTENTS

★   ★   ★   ★

ACKNOWLEDGMENTS

★   ★   ★   ★   ★

Thanks to:

Saul Bass, Pol Bury, Joe Budne, Baldo Diodato, Madame DUCHAMP, Erik Gronborg, Don Hazlitt, Ludovico de Luigi, Irva Mandelbaum, Fred Marcellino, Bertha Mole, Peter Passuntino, Farwell Perry, Rocky Pinciotti, Michel Proulx, Ben Schonzeit, Edward Sorel, Laura Wilensky, and Tomi Ungerer.

Bonnie Aiffa, Marlborough Gallery; Carol Celantano, Phyllis Kind Gallery; Kathleen Cullen, Pace Gallery; Muldoon Elder, Vorpal Gallery; Terry Hubscher, Marlborough Gallery; F. Joan Goldberg, Fine Art Acquisitions Ltd.; Louis Jewel, Peter Max Enterprises; Vivian Linaus, Cityarts Workshop; Lisa Martizia, Castelli Gallery; Russet Lederman, David Mc Kee, Inc.; Elizabeth Robbs, Sotheby Parke Bernet; Nathan Segal, Booz's Gallery; Michael Solomon, Spencer & Samuels, Inc.; Kenneth Walker, Max Protech Gallery.

Eric Ashworth, Ralph Babcock, Risa Chalfin, Candida Donadio, Tamar Gordon, David Luder, Lucy Painter, Eileen Savel, Muriel Steinberg, Sheri Sussman, Josephine Vela, Sam Wiener, and Leonard Wasserman.

Peggy Barber, American Library Association; Ada Cone, Reader Mail, *New York Daily News;* Mary Danakas, Greek Orthodox Archdiocese of North and South America; Wilbur Daniels, ILGWU; Diana Elkins, Condé Nast Publications, Inc.; Spencer Falk, Pfizer, Inc.; Celia Fink, Women Strike for Peace; Patricia Fishler, Embassy Pictures; Thomas Fowler, the Ad Council; Steven Friedman, El Al Airlines; William Gaines, *Mad* magazine; Sally Gervirtz, Twentieth Century-Fox; George Grau, RCA Records; Ronnie Grillo, Luckie & Forney Advertising; Leslie Griswold, Pushpin Lubalin Peckolick; Raymond Gross, Jr., Stroh Brewery, Inc.; Joan Hafey, Young & Rubicam; David Hawthorne, *Millimeter* magazine; Yasuo Harada, Toshiba; John Howliss, Brooklyn Academy of Music; Mary T. Howell, Young & Rubicam; the Rev. Thomas U. Jung; Archer Kine, New York Art Directors Club; Ari Korpivaara, American Civil Liberties Union; Frank and Jeff Lavaty, Lavaty Studio; Kyung Hak Lee, *Korean News;* Duana Le May, Cosimo's Studio, Inc.; Bara Levin, Chemical Bank, Ann Lowen, Friends Seminary; John Mancini, I.S. 96; John E. Mara, AFL-CIO; Jonathan Martin, Thorn EMI; Joyce McCray, Friends Seminary; Gloria Melo, TAP Air Portugal; Sid Merians, Talon, Inc.; Jose Ortiz, OOSPAAL; Dr. Fathi Osmani, Arabia, the *Islamic World Review;* Janice Penino, WNBC-AM 66; Sally Pomeroy, Marvel Comics Group; Kenneth Powell, A&M Records; Peggy Raphi, Cinecom; Annabel Robson, Fontana Paperbacks; Barbara Rochman, NOW New York City; Shari Rosenfeld, the Greater New York Conference on Soviet Jewry; Warwick Ross, Seven Keys Films Pty. Ltd.; Ann Sandhorst, Pantheon Books; Norton Sandlor, Socialist Workers party; Bernie Shapiro, Chester Gore Co., Inc.; Lucianna Sowaal, FIAT; Martin Szymanski, Stroh Brewery Co.; C. M. Ullman, Campbell Soup Co.; Michael Wilkins, Stanford Chaparral.

INTRODUCTION

★　　　★　　　★　　　★　　　★

The urge to collect is not easily controlled. It strikes capriciously, without warning or apparent reasons; one day a devoted family man, the next a passionate hoarder of netsukes, or stones, or beer cans, or signed first editions.

In my early years I had no particular interest in the Statue of Liberty. I first visited her as a Cub Scout and with the more adventurous members of the troop climbed to her crown. The trip was uneventful, except for a bloody nose received by one of my fellow scouts. We all disagreed as to the number of steps to her crown, but never thought enough about it to find out the correct answer. For years after that she remained someone I saw only in passing, as the subway took me over the Manhattan Bridge. She had her life and I had mine.

I next visited her as an adult, on the eve of my departure for California. Visiting the city's landmarks was my way of saying goodbye. I had a great day. The weather was warm for October, so the ferry trip from Battery Park to Liberty Island was a complete delight.

There had been many changes at the statue since my last visit. The grounds had been landscaped and were well tended. In the statue's base I found a museum devoted to the history of immigration to this country. I climbed to her crown and this time counted 171 steps. From there I waved goodbye to the city of my birth.

I moved to California and settled in, but often thought of the pleasant day I'd spent at the statue. One night I awoke from a dream that had starred the Statue of Liberty. She was renamed Ms. Liberty, and when the one-billionth hot dog dropped in her crown she said, "Enough is enough. After all these years of greeting everyone to these shores, you'd think they'd remember with a call, or at least a card. They should live and be well, but what about me?"

So she hopped the next ferry to the city and became a New York glitterati, seen at all the right places. An opening or party wasn't complete unless she was there. She always beamed for the paparazzi, and soon was appearing on the cover of *People* magazine. Goldwyn wanted her for a six-figure deal out on the Coast. When she left New York, the *Daily News* ran a banner headline: Liberty: "Drop Dead, N.Y."

She ended up signing with Columbia Records and toured the world as Brassy, lead singer of the punk-rock group the Monumentals.

In Paris, Rodin's *Thinker* declared his love.

In Japan she was greeted by the emperor.

In Washington she was denounced on the floor of the Senate.

Moscow accused her of capitalistic intentions to undermine the world's youth.

Hurt by this criticism, she went to India and visited the maharishi.

She returned to California to actualize her potential, and strange things happened at the fat farm.

After being Rolfed, she consulted an astrologer, who helped her to decide upon a proper livelihood. She marketed *thachkes* of herself and returned to New York dressed for success as the president of Liberty Corporation.

Much shook up after an assassination attempt, she was last seen taking a Checker cab to an unknown destination.

★　　　　★　　　　★

After this dream I began to see images of her everywhere—on book covers, in advertisements in galleries. I innocently began to collect these images, and soon it was a consuming passion. I searched through libraries, museums, and bookstores. I attended meetings of postcard collectors, went to toy stores and stands that sold stamps, all with one intention: to find images of her.

I read history books about her and found them incomplete since they stop telling her story in 1886, the year of her dedication. I unearthed details and anecdotes about her that I felt were mine alone. I filled in the years from 1886 to the present.

Everything I've found—history, anecdotes, arcane trivia, and images of the statue herself—is contained in this volume. I hope it pleases you as it has me.

IMAGES OF LIBERTY

★   ★   ★   ★   ★

Chapter 1

HISTORY OF
LIBERTY

★　　　★　　　★　　　★　　　★

The most visited personality in the United States, the Statue of Liberty has stood in New York Harbor since 1886. As the most recognizable symbol of what this country believes in and stands for, she has inspired people throughout the world to political and artistic activity.

We are a country of immigrants, many of whom saw the statue as their first sight of this land. Stories about her have been passed down through the generations like treasured family heirlooms. She's not just a copper, steel, and stone monument to be thought of on national holidays—she is America itself, a land of people with numerous countries of origin, various religions and racial groups.

There are many myths about the statue that have come to be accepted as historical fact. The foremost myth is that the statue was given to America in a spontaneous outpouring of public generosity by the French people to celebrate the United States' centennial and to honor the historic ties of French-American friendship. The gift was actually made as an act of political propaganda aimed at influencing the structure of the French state.

France, from the early 1800s to the end of the century, was politically unstable. There was a continual struggle for power between the monarchists, who wished to have a king as the head of state, and the Republicans, who desired a more representative form of government. When the monarchy was restored in 1815, it set in motion, through repressive measures, revolutionary forces that erupted in 1830, 1848, and 1871. Throughout this time it was unsafe to voice opinions that opposed the government's viewpoint. Thus the French Republicans, led by Edouard-René Lefebvre de Laboulaye, decided to use allegorical tales and symbolic actions as a safe means of expressing their criticism.

The idea for the statue was proposed at a dinner party hosted by Laboulaye and attended by leading French Republicans and the sculptor who eventually created her, Frédéric Auguste Bartholdi. Laboulaye had decided that some grand gesture was needed to advance the cause of French republicanism, and what better way to achieve this than by ideologically aligning France, by way of a gift, with the United States, the most politically progressive country in the world? America in 1886 was the only country that had a constitutional form of government. The gift of the statue was designed to highlight the differences between the two countries' forms of government. The statue was originally named Liberty Enlightening the World and positioned to face Europe, not America, because she was envisioned as symbolically spreading liberty from America to France.

Bartholdi, if not the most artistically creative sculptor of the time, was the ideal person to do the job. A French patriot, he helped to defend his native town of Colmar, in Alsace, when it was invaded by the Prussians during the Franco-Prussian War. He later became an aide-de-camp to General Garibaldi during the Italian patriot's attempt to lead an army against Prussia.

Fig. 1 (right). Florine Stettheimer, *New York City Harbor,* 1918. *Courtesy Richard Feigen Gallery, N.Y.*

4

LIBERTY

NEW YORK
1913

Fig. 2. Ben Schonzeit, *Yankee Flame*, 1975. *Courtesy of the artist.*

It's possible that Bartholdi's wartime experiences are what led him to be a sculptor of monuments. In any case, his love for the colossal showed early in his career as a sculptor. At the age of nineteen in 1855, his first sculpture was exhibited at the Paris Salon. It was of a famous military leader from the Alsace region, General Rapp. Since it had been commissioned by the city of Colmar to celebrate one of its most glorious natives, it made sense to have Bartholdi, also a native son, sculpt the piece. Bartholdi's monument to General Rapp was 3.5 meters high and stood on a pedestal of 4.2 meters. It was too big to fit inside the Paris Salon and was given a prominent place outside, where it gained much attention and critical approval.

In 1856 Bartholdi went on an extended trip to Egypt. He had known of the colossal statues of the ancient past—the Zeus of Phidias, the Chryselephantine Athena, and, largest of all, the Colossus of Rhodes, but on this trip he saw colossal sculptures for the first time. He also saw the colossi at Thebes and much admired them.

The Statue of Liberty was not Bartholdi's first colossal sculpture project. In 1867 he approached Ismail Pasha, the ruler of Egypt who was visiting France in conjunction with the Universal Exposition, with a plan to erect a colossal statue at the entrance of the newly completed Suez Canal. The sculpture was to have been a gigantic woman holding aloft a torch symbolizing "progress" and "Egypt enlightening Asia." It would represent Ismail's efforts to westernize his land and would commemorate the achievement of the building of the canal. The statue would also have served as a functional lighthouse.

Bartholdi's sketches and clay models of *Egypt Enlightening Asia* bear great similarity in design to the Statue of Liberty, he later insisted that the similarity in design was purely coincidental.

Laboulaye and Bartholdi had been discussing the possibility of the Statue of Liberty since 1865. When they made their plans known to other leading French Republi-

cans at the dinner party in 1870, it was decided that the time was right for Bartholdi to make an exploratory trip to America and see what sort of reaction this project would evoke.

In 1871 Bartholdi was in America. He met and publicized his project with potential financial backers, newspaper publishers, the famous abolitionist Senator Sumner, and President Ulysses S. Grant. He informed his

Fig. 3. Ludovico de Luigi, *New Liberty of Venice*, 1976. *Courtesy of the artist.*

confederates back in France that his plans were being warmly received and that congressional approval for the statue would be easy to obtain. He also told them that he had found the ideal site for the statue, Bedloe's Island, in New York Harbor.

Bartholdi returned to France to work on the final model of the statue. The political climate, however, was deemed inappropriate for revealing their grand

Fig. 4. Peter Max, *Statue of Liberty #6*, © Peter Max 1981. From the Peter Max Statue of Liberty series of six statues painted at the White House, July 4, 1981.

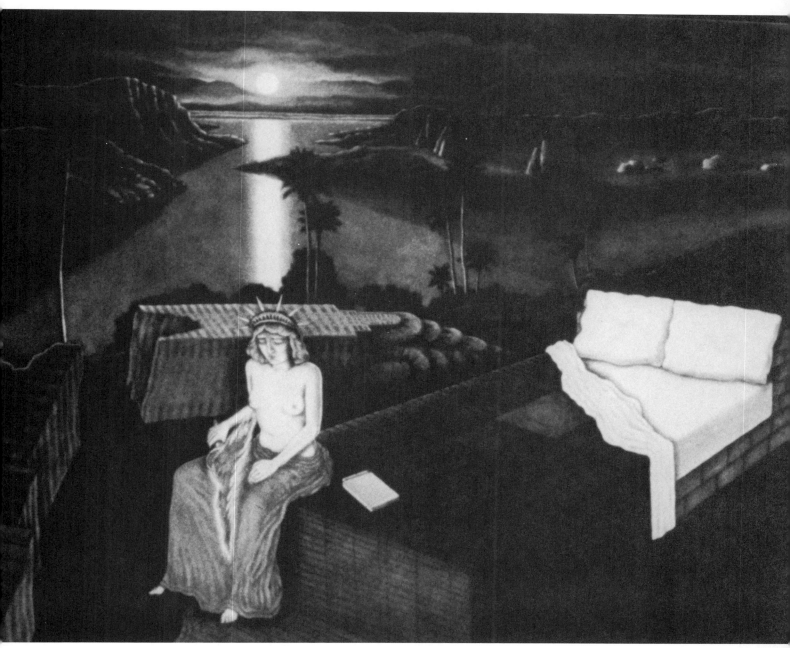

Fig. 5. Rem Koolhaas and Madelon Vriesendorp, *New Jersey,*
1975. *Courtesy Max Protech Gallery, N.Y.*

project, so Bartholdi and the Republicans decided to test their idea by using a less politically explosive sculpture as their first gift to America. In 1873 Bartholdi was commissioned to make a larger-than-life bronze statue of Lafayette for presentation to the city of New York as a gesture of thanks to that city and to America for the aid supplied to Paris after the siege of 1870–71. A plaster version of the sculpture was exhibited in the Paris Salon of 1873 and was warmly received. Lafayette was a French national hero and his support of the Republicans against George IV was so far in the past that the political statement did not seem very threatening. It did not have to be interpreted in contemporary terms but could be seen as honoring a patriot who fought against the traditional enemy of the French, the English.

The final bronze version of the sculpture was erected in New York City's Union Square in 1876. It still stands there, serving as a reminder of the park's former days of glory when it functioned very much as a town green, where orators would come and stand on boxes to speak on the issues of the day.

In 1874, when moderate Republicans had gained effective control of France, it seemed the appropriate time to announce the planned gift to America of Bartholdi's statue of Liberty Enlightening the World. A French-American Union was established in 1875 to raise funds and coordinate publicity for the project on both sides of the Atlantic. Laboulaye headed the French committee, William Evarts the American committee. A large dinner to celebrate the project was held at the Hotel du Louvre on November 6, 1875, and was attended by a wide range of politicians comprising the complete spectrum of French political thought.

The next task for Laboulaye and the Franco-American Union was to raise funds for the statue. Businessmen with ties to the United States donated a sizable amount to the project, but nowhere near the needed amount. The major appeal was made to French city governments that traditionally had financed the

Fig. 6. Ludovic Booz,
Statue of Liberty. Courtesy
Booz's Gallery, North Miami.

building of monuments. A few cities, including Paris and Le Havre, responded, as did the Freemason Society. A total of 200,000 francs was raised through these sources, a large sum, but still far short of what was needed. The municipal governments saw very little reason to contribute to something that would be thousands of miles away.

On April 25, 1876, a benefit performance of Charles Gounod's cantata *La Liberté Éclairant le Monde* was held at the Paris Opera, but it was poorly attended, netting only 8,000 francs. Obviously it was going to take much longer than originally anticipated to raise the necessary funds.

The statue's right arm, holding its torch, was sent to America and exhibited at the 1876 Philadelphia Centennial celebration. The statue's head was exhibited

Fig. 7. Martinique, *Liberty.* © *1984 Fine Art Acquisitions, Ltd.*

Plate 1. Frank Riley, *Joy Stick Skyline*, N.Y.

Courtesy of the artist

Plate 2. Luis Jimenez, *Barfly*, 1973

Courtesy Phyllis Kind Gallery, N.Y.

Plate 3. Mimi Gross, *Ms. Liberty*, From Red Grooms and Mimi Gross's
Ruckus Manhattan, 1975, in Collaboration with the Ruckus Construction Co.
Base by Connie Harris

Courtesy Marlborough Gallery, N.Y.

Plate 4. Roger Brown, *Liberty Inviting Artists to Take Part in an Exhibition Against
International Leftist Terrorism* (IRA/PLO/FALN/Red Brigade/Sandinistas/Bulgarians), 1983
Courtesy Phyllis Kind Gallery, N.Y.

Plate 5. Saul Steinberg, *Ship of State*, 1959

Pace Gallery, N.Y.

Plate 6. Ivan Kustura, *Reclining Figure/Post Atomic*, 1983

Courtesy Vorpal Gallery, N.Y. and S.F.

Plate 7. Erte, *Liberty, Fearless and Free*

Plate 8. Roy Lichtenstein, *Paintings with Statue of Liberty,* 1983

Courtesy Castelli Gallery, N.Y.

at the Paris International Fair of 1878. Both parts of the statue were chosen for exhibition because they were the most impressive components and each allowed visitors to enter and climb to a viewing platform.

In 1879 Laboulaye and the other members of the Franco-American Union realized that in order to raise the full amount needed for the statue's construction, they would have to appeal to a much larger group of potential donors. They decided to have a lottery, and prevailed upon numerous firms to donate 538 prizes. With the chance of winning something, the French people enthusiastically supported the project, and 300,000 tickets were sold. On July 7, 1881, a celebration dinner was held. Laboulaye and the Union had raised the equivalent of $400,000, enough to complete the statue. Storytellers

Fig. 9. Laura Wilensky, *July 4th Weekend*, ceramic plate. From the collection of Tommy Simpson/Missy Stevens. *Courtesy of the artist.*

still say that the statue's copper body is composed of the melted-down centimes donated by French schoolchildren.

Since the statue had gained such great public acceptance, the Republicans chanced something very risky. They had Bartholdi erect the statue first at his Paris workshop before dismantling her for shipment to America. The danger lay in the fact that the political climate could have changed and a monarchist government could have come to power. Under these circumstances, being associated with a gigantic statue towering over the city proclaiming "liberty" could have meant death.

In 1885, when she was dismantled and shipped to America, her absence from Paris was definitely felt— so much so that a replica one-fourth the size of the original was later erected on the Seine at the Ile des Cygnes, in view of the Eiffel Tower.

Making the statue was harder than raising the money for it. While the original plaster model was slightly over four feet in height, the statue itself would be 151 feet. The first plans had the surface of the statue made of hammered sheets of bronze. Realizing bronze would be too heavy, Bartholdi substituted pure copper, $3/32$ of an inch thick. Alexandre-Gustave Eiffel proposed that the exterior surface be fastened to an interior iron framework, which would provide the structural strength needed to keep the statue erect.

Enlargements of the original model were made, first to one-sixteenth and to one-fourth the ultimate size. Fine wires led from 300 important points on the second enlarged model to 1,200 points on four plaster sections that united would form the final statue. Using this new copy, workers fitted boards that became latticed molds against which other workers hammered the copper sheets into the desired form. This procedure yielded hundreds of formed copper sheets, which were later hung upon the iron framework designed by Eiffel.

The statue was not built from the toes upward. Different sections were made according to Bartholdi's

Fig. 10. Rocky Pinciotti, *Liberty*, 1982, neon sculpture. *Courtesy of the artist.*

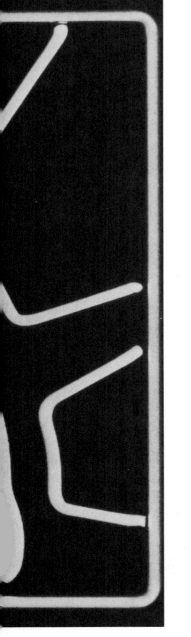

preference for working on them, and the head and the right arm with the torch were done early to provide recognizable pieces for exhibition. Every Sunday hundreds of Parisians gathered in the yards of Gaget, Gauthier et Cie., where the statue was being built, to watch the monument take form.

In the early part of 1884, the work was completed. On July 4, 1884, a presentation ceremony was held, formally giving the statue to the United States.

Fig. 11. Erik Gronborg, porcelain cup, 1976.

The next task was to dismantle the statue and transport her to America. It took months of labor to take the statue apart, carefully label each piece, and securely pack them away. Forty-nine large wooden cases were needed to store all the copper sheets that comprised the external surface, and thirty-six cases more were used for the internal iron structure. Special trucks transported the 500,000 pounds of metal and wood to the Gare St.-Lazare. From there a train of seventy cars carried the

Fig. 12 (above). Ms. Liberty, neon sign. Photographer Michel Proulx.

Fig. 13 (right). Tomie Arai, Women Hold Up Half the Sky. © 1974 Cityarts Workshop.

Fig. 14 (this page). Irva Mandelbaum, *Happy Birthday Liberty.* © 1984 IRVA.

Fig. 15 (next page). Late nineteenth-century weathervane, J.L. Mott Ironworks. *Courtesy Sotheby Parke Bernet*

statue to the French port of Rouen. In May 1885 the statue left Rouen aboard the warship *Isere* on its voyage across the Atlantic to its new home, America.

The responsibility for providing a site for the statue was America's. The famous Civil War commander General William T. Sherman represented the U.S. government in dealings with Bartholdi and the Franco-American Union. The choice of construction sites had been narrowed down to two federal properties in New York Harbor: Bedloe's Island and Governors Island.

General Sherman favored Governors Island, believing the statue could better serve as a lighthouse from there. Had Governors Island been chosen, the statue would have had to face America, thereby defeating the original idea— America shining the torch of liberty toward France. General Sherman acquiesced to Bartholdi's desires and Bedloe's Island became the statue's new home.

The funds for the pedestal were to come from public contributions of the American people, but donations were even further from the necessary amount than the French had been in their initial fund-raising drive for the statue. Indeed the statue itself was not greeted as warmly as Bartholdi had led his fellow Frenchmen to believe she would be. America was somewhat wary of France, keenly aware of France's aggressive activities as a colonial power. In recent times it had added Algeria to its holdings and expanded greatly in Indochina (Vietnam) and Tunisia. The International Expositions in Paris in 1855, 1867, and 1878 were held to let the world know about France's eminence in culture, science, and technology. At least three-quarters of the world's Catholic missionary priests at the time were French. Had the term been in use back then, the gift of the statue could very easily have been labeled an example of French cultural imperialism. The feeling was that America was developing a culture of its own; why help pay for a French sculpture that would serve as a reminder of France's eminent position in the world?

New York City volunteered to help finance the building of the pedestal, and a bill was introduced in the New York State legislature that would allow the city to do so. That bill, however, was vetoed by New York's governor, Grover Cleveland. Ironically, two years later he would play an instrumental part in the statue's dedication ceremonies in his next governmental office, as president of the United States.

Bills introduced in both houses of Congress would have authorized the federal government to spend $100,000 on the construction of the statue's pedestal.

Fig. 16. Baldo Diodato, *Italian Lyric*, 1983. *Courtesy of the artist.*

Fig. 17. Peter Passuntino, *Christ Entering New York City*, 1971.
Courtesy of the artist.

The measures were defeated because the project was viewed as benefiting New York and not the rest of the country. The general feeling was that since New York was the business and cultural center of the country, it should be able to pay for the project itself. The federal government did agree to pay for the dedication ceremonies and future upkeep of the statue because it would be a functioning lighthouse.

It looked as if the statue might not be erected on Bedloe's Island since the money for the pedestal was not coming in and no new sources of revenue seemed likely. Other cities—including Baltimore, Boston, Minneapolis, Philadelphia, and San Francisco—offered to provide a suitable home for the statue if New York was unable to.

Happily for New York, in 1883 Joseph Pulitzer, publisher of the *New York World,* took up the cause of raising the needed funds. He used his paper to criticize New York's many millionaires who spent so much on their lavish life-styles while neglecting this cause. Daily he printed the names of every donor who contributed more than a dollar to the fund.

Fig. 18. Peter Passuntino, *American Still Life*, 1974. *Courtesy of the artist.*

Fig. 19. Pol Bury, Untitled. 1984. *Courtesy of the artist.*

Fig. 20. Amy Dresner, *Out to Lunch*, 1985. *Courtesy of the artist.*

Fig. 21. CPLY, *1984 and All That*, 1984. *Courtesy Phyllis Kind Gallery, N.Y.*

Fig. 22. Oscar de Mejo, *Dr. Merck Visits New York.* Courtesy Merck & Co., Rahway, N.J.

In 1885, when sufficient money had still not been raised, he renewed his efforts with even greater enthusiasm. He staged a massive public-relations campaign that prompted over 120,000 people to donate to the construction fund. He printed prominently in his newspaper letters from schoolchildren, aged widows, and poor office workers, all of whom were willingly donating whatever they could to the cause.

Work progressed quickly on the construction of the pedestal designed by the American architect Richard M. Hunt. When completed, the pedestal stood eighty-nine feet high. The statue raised upon it was another 151 feet. Together they loom majestically in New York Harbor. In the statue's raised right hand is a torch, the beacon of liberty. In her left arm is a slate engraved with

the Roman numerals for July 4, 1776, the date of America's independence. She treads on broken shackles showing Liberty's ability to destroy tyranny.

On October 26, 1886, the dedication ceremonies were held. It was a damp, chilly day, but that did not lessen the excitement and enthusiasm of the crowd as they watched the ceremonies. Thanks to Pulitzer's public-relations campaign, the American people had finally

Fig. 23. Katherine Porter, Untitled, 1983. *Courtesy David McKee, Inc., N.Y.*

taken the statue to heart. The ceremonies were presided over by President Grover Cleveland and attended by officials of both the United States and France. When all the speeches were completed, the torch of Liberty Enlightening the World was lit. It has continued to shine, with only short interludes of interrupted service, from then on. That evening, as part of ceremonies, there was a great fireworks display to celebrate the statue.

Over the years there have been many proposals to alter the statue, but, fortunately, few changes have been made. The first change in the statue was a welcome one. In 1903 a poem by Emma Lazarus, a German-American Jew, was immortalized by being inscribed on a plaque at the statue's base. Entitled *The New Colossus,* the poem was a welcome addition because it eloquently expressed what the statue had come to mean to America and the world. Instead of being a beacon of liberty to France, the statue was a welcoming light for this land, inviting entry to all who sought freedom and the opportunity for a better life.

> *Give me your tired, your poor,*
> *Your huddled masses yearning to breathe free,*
> *The wretched refuse of your teeming shore.*
> *Send these, the homeless, tempest-tost to me.*
> *I lift my lamp beside the golden door!*

The next proposal to change the statue was not as welcome, and luckily a mass public outcry prevented it from happening. In 1906 the federal government proposed to paint the statue's exterior. Her natural copper green patina, because of the public's vociferous outrage, was preserved.

In 1915 Joseph Pennell, one of the era's most celebrated artists, proposed moving the statue from its site on Bedloe's Island to Governors Island. He also proposed that its base be heightened so the statue could better function as a lighthouse. He argued that once placed on Governors Island, the Statue of Liberty would make the entrance to New York the most monumental and magnificent in the world. Pennell's proposal is not, however, the reason he will forever be associated with the statue. He created a poster of her that was used to sell Liberty Loan War Bonds during World War I. Pennell's poster "That Liberty Shall Not Perish from the Earth" was the most popular poster of the time and raised much money for the war effort. Indeed, the poster

Fig. 24. David Smith, *Medals for Dishonor: The Fourth Estate.*
© 1939. Collection Candida and Rebecca Smith. *Courtesy*
Marlborough Gallery, N.Y.

Fig. 25. Reginald Marsh, mural, *U.S. Custom House on Bowling Green, N.Y.,* 1937.

was in such great demand that he wrote a best-selling book about it.

The next proposal to change the statue came in 1920 from an American minister who suggested that she be replaced with a colossal statue of Jesus Christ. The American press gave very little attention to the idea, but the French newspapers were quite offended by the suggestion. Commented one: "We could understand a statue of a dry American holding a bible and surrounded by customs officials. We would accept the project of a colossal cowboy, dancing girl, Dempsey or Rockefeller—in short anything very 'exciting'—but a statue of Christ, so poor among the poor, erected at the entrance of the country of the dollar and the temple of money? No."

The next proposal was for a change not of statues but of status. In 1924 President Calvin Coolidge proclaimed the Statue of Liberty a national monument.

Also in 1924, the son of a Swiss immigrant offered to donate and maintain a wristwatch for the statue. The watch would have had a large luminous dial visible from shore, turning the statue into New York's own Big Ben. This gift was turned down by the Department of War, the federal agency then responsible for the statue's upkeep, because "If permitted to have a wristwatch, fashionable modistes would be showering her with gowns, and beauty specialists persuading her to indulge in nine varieties of haircuts."

In 1937 the spikes of the statue's crown were removed and rebuilt, and over the years the copper sheets of the torch have been replaced by tinted cathedral glass to heighten the brightness of her beacon. For the same reason different light sources have been used to illuminate the torch, most recently high-intensity incandescent 1,000-watt bulbs. For the duration of World War II, her beacon was turned off. It was lit again on May 8, 1945, to celebrate VE (Victory in Europe) Day.

The statue's interior was painted in 1945 with an enamel specially developed to be impervious to lipstick. Visitors had been covering the interior surfaces with

lipstick signatures, which ate through the existing coating to the copper underneath. A special lipstick remover was also developed to easily remove signatures as they appeared.

In 1953 a lawsuit was filed that tried to have New Jersey declared the statue's home. The suit contended that since Bedloe's Island was surrounded by Jersey territorial waters, the island and its famous inhab-

Fig. 26 (left). Robert Rauschenberg, *Estate,* 1963. *Courtesy Castelli Gallery, N.Y.*

Fig. 27 (right). Farwell Perry, *Statue of Liberty,* 1983. *Courtesy of the artist.*

Fig. 28. Cosimo Scianna, *Crying Liberty.* Courtesy Cosimo's Studio, Inc.

The Wanderer finds Liberty in America

Fig. 29. Golda Meir, 1919,
Milwaukee, Wisconsin.

Fig. 30 (left page). Marcel Duchamp, André Breton as the Statue of Liberty, 1946.

Fig. 31 (this page). Ed Sorel, Richard Nixon giving the finger to the GI Bill of Rights, 1974.

itant were part of New Jersey, not New York. The suit was brought by the owner of the refreshment-and-souvenir concession on the island. She was seeking the return of all the sales tax she had paid to New York City, since there was no sales tax in New Jersey. New Jersey, as a matter of local pride, joined in the suit and argued its case for ownership of the island. The courts, however, were definite in their decision, ruling the Statue of Liberty was a New Yorker due to a treaty signed by both states in the 1800s that ceded the island to New York.

In 1956 Miss Liberty's home was given a new name. By an act of Congress, Bedloe's Island was re-named Liberty Island. The same bill established the Immigration Museum that would be housed in the statue's base and be devoted to preserving the cultural heritage of America's immigrants.

Meanwhile, New Jersey residents have continued to lay claim to the statue. In 1962 a New Jersey

congressman introduced legislation in the House of Representatives that called for the construction of a footbridge between Liberty Island and the Jersey City shore. The bridge never came about because the Department of the Interior, the federal agency now responsible for the statue's maintenance, opposed the idea, on the

Fig. 32. Statue of Liberty on the Pont de Grenelle Bridge in Paris, France. *Photo courtesy French Cultural Services.*

grounds that it "would destroy the scenic character of Liberty Island and detract from the present dignity and impressiveness of the Statue of Liberty."

The Jersey City Chamber of Commerce held a meeting at the Statue of Liberty in 1966 to publicize New Jersey's claim to Liberty Island. They passed a resolution demanding that Jersey City be included as part of the

Fig. 33 (left). World War II Times Square asbestos Statue of Liberty, New York City.

Plate 9.   Richard Lindner, *Out of Towners,* 1968

Spencer & Samuels Co., N.Y.

Plate 10. James Morlock

AMERICANA

STANFORD

Chaparral

One Buck   Dec 1980

Plate 11.   Stanford Chaparral, Dec. 1980, Artist Bruce Handy

Courtesy Stanford Chaparral

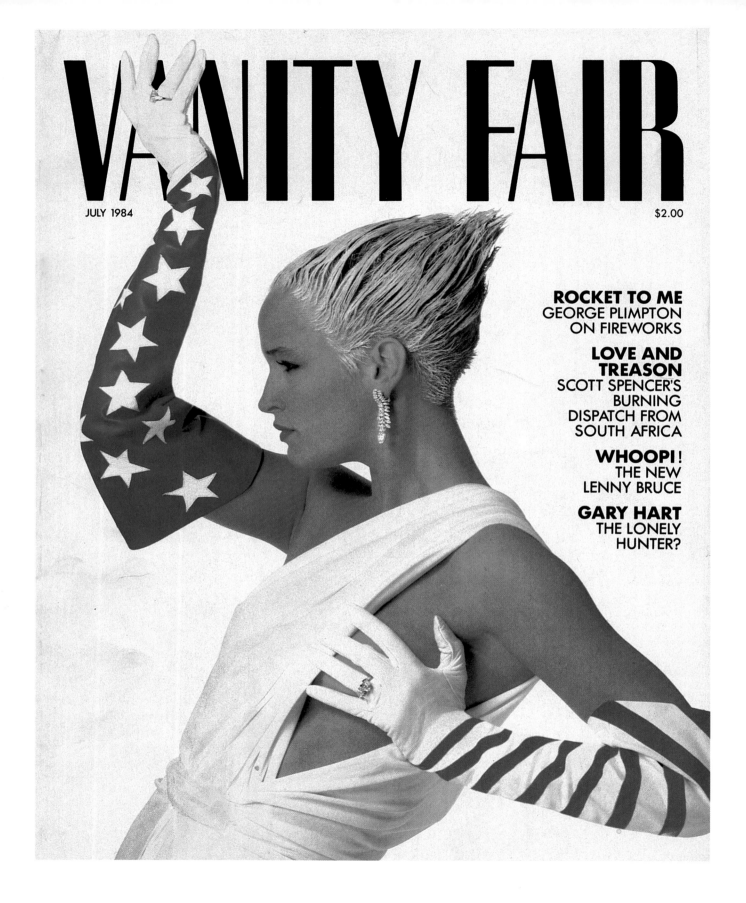

VANITY FAIR

JULY 1984

$2.00

ROCKET TO ME
GEORGE PLIMPTON
ON FIREWORKS

**LOVE AND
TREASON**
SCOTT SPENCER'S
BURNING
DISPATCH FROM
SOUTH AFRICA

WHOOPI!
THE NEW
LENNY BRUCE

GARY HART
THE LONELY
HUNTER?

Plate 12. Vanity Fair, July 1984, Photograph by Bill King

©*1984 Condé Nast Publications, Inc., Courtesy* Vanity Fair

Plate 13. "Mr. Liberty" photo by Michael Rock

©1980 Rockshots

Plate 14.   *Time* magazine ad, 1983

Courtesy Time *magazine*

Plate 15. Turn-of-the-century ads, Chemical Bank Archives

Courtesy Chemical Bank

Plate 16. Fred Marcellino, *March for the Dream*, 1983

Courtesy of the artist

official postal address of the island; that the New Jersey telephone company provide a toll-free line to the island for New Jersey residents; that regular passenger ferry service be provided between the island and Jersey City; and that the Department of the Interior give equal recognition to Jersey City and New York City in regard to Liberty Island.

In 1971 a New Jersey legislator sent a cable to the president of France urging him to put the French-made statue "on a swivel so that the residents of Jersey City can get a front view once in a while" since his constituents "had been afforded a rear unemotional view of Miss Liberty's shape since the statue was put in New York Harbor."

Figs. 34, 35, 36 Boy Scout Statue of Liberty in front of the state capitol at Cheyenne, Wyoming; Boy Scout Statue of Liberty in St. Joseph, Missouri; Boy Scout Statue of Liberty in North Kansas City, Missouri.

Fig. 37. Statue of Liberty atop Liberty National Insurance Co.,
Birmingham, Alabama.

Since then, Liberty Park has been constructed on the Jersey City shore. It is a beautiful public space with carefully tended grounds and has become an outdoor cultural center. Regular ferry service was instituted between the park and Liberty Island, a much shorter trip than from Battery Park in New York City. Unfortunately, due to lack of demand, the service to Liberty Island from Liberty Park was suspended in 1984.

In 1985 New Jersey once again claimed the statue as its own. The matter is in the courts.

The most radical plan to alter the Statue of Liberty came from the political group called the Black Liberation Front. They were arrested in 1965 for plotting to blow her up. Thirty sticks of dynamite were found in their possession, which army experts said "were enough to blow the top off the statue."

In 1975, after a joint House-Senate bill to provide humanitarian aid to South Vietnamese refugees was defeated, a member of Congress proposed that the words of Emma Lazarus's poem, inscribed on the statue's base, be changed from the original to read:

Do not give me your tired, your poor,
The wretched refuse of your teeming shores who will further
depress the job market.
Rather send back these homeless and tempest tossed, to where
they came from,
While I make sure the golden door is firmly shut and solidly on
its hinges.

The statue has changed the most during a comprehensive rehabilitation that took place between 1983 and 1986 in anticipation of the statue's one-hundredth birthday in 1986. After 100 years of standing in New York Harbor, the Statue of Liberty has been restored to a state that will enable her to easily be the beacon of liberty for another hundred years. The restoration was accomplished under the auspices of the Statue of Liberty–Ellis

Fig. 38. Theatre de Poche, Brussels, poster for the play *Macbird*, 1968. Artist Jacques Richez AGI.

Fig. 39. Millimeter magazine cover, June 1982.

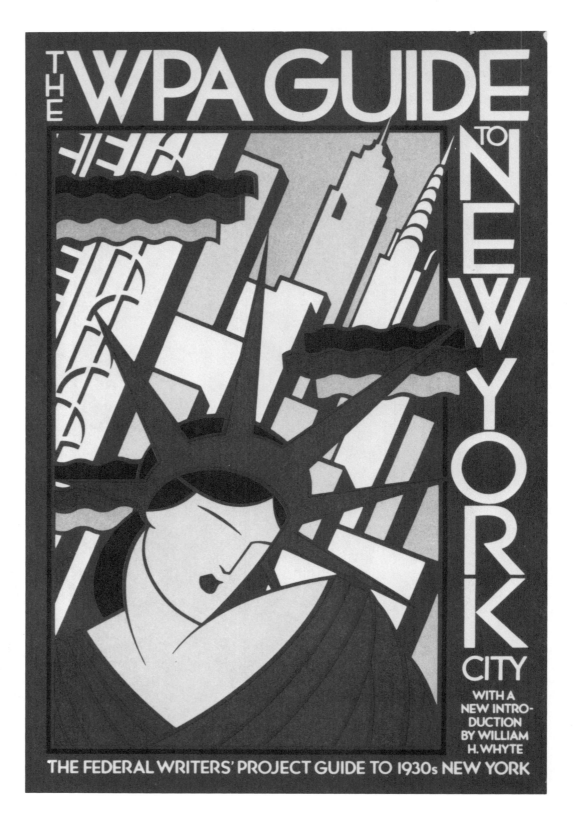

THE FEDERAL WRITERS' PROJECT GUIDE TO 1930s NEW YORK

Fig. 40 (this page). The WPA Guide to New York City. Artist John Martinez. Pantheon Books, a division of Random House. © *1982, Random House.*

Fig. 41 (right page). Mad magazine, #252, Jan. 1983. Artist Armanli. © 1984 E.C. Publications.

Island Centennial Commission, headed by Lee A. Iacocca, chairman of the Chrysler Corporation.

The renovation of the statue included replacing part of the torch above the walkway. This was done by Gaget, Gauthier et Cie., of Paris, France—the same firm that made the statue a century ago. The same construction methods were used in making the new torch as were used in making the original.

The viewing area in the crown has been improved, and closed-circuit television cameras have been installed so people with physical limitations and those not wanting to make the climb will be able to enjoy the view from the crown while remaining below.

The structural skeleton in the right shoulder has been entirely rebuilt. All loose and missing rivets, which hold the copper sheeting to the support system, have been replaced. Her exterior has been cleaned and coated with an anticorrosive agent. Her entire internal framework has been replaced and made stronger by the use of a corrosion-proof alloy.

The stairway to the crown has been widened, as have the rest platforms along the way. An elevator has been installed that goes from the museum, in the statue's base, up to the arm. It is used for emergencies and for continuing maintenance of the statue. There is also now an elevator in the pedestal, allowing greater access for people with physical disabilities.

Another level of the pedestal has been made accessible to the public. The interior and exterior lighting of the statue has been completely redone. There is better ventilation throughout the Statue, making it a more comfortable place to visit.

The restoration was not limited entirely to the statue herself; improvements were made throughout Liberty Island. Much-needed work was done on the administration and concession buildings, a new dock shelter was built, and the grounds were relandscaped.

Just as the original funding for the statue's base came from public donations, so have the funds for

Fig. 42. Arabia: The Islamic World Review, Sept. 1984. Artist Mustafa Aksay

restoration. The money was raised in various ways: schoolchildren selling candy, donation drives by labor unions, fraternal and civic organizations. Corporations acted as official sponsors of the restoration and donated percentages of their sales to the fund. I have included in this book a representative group of ads from companies that were official sponsors of the restoration; their ads all carry the official centennial logo. The American public responded very generously to the cause, as did the people of France.

The statue has a history of political significance, and it's not surprising that she is constantly used as a staging ground for political protest. The first occurred in 1926: Three members of the World War Veterans Light

Wine and Beer League, angered at being denied permission to testify before the Senate Judiciary Committee's hearings on Prohibition, draped two sixty-foot black crepe banners from the statue's crown. This event set the stage for many more to follow.

The next incident occurred in 1956, when a Hungarian immigrant broke open the door that leads to the statue's arm and hung both American and Hungarian flags from Liberty's torch to protest the Soviet Union's armed invasion of Hungary.

In 1957, members of the New York Committee of the Movement of the 26th of July, supporters of the Cuban revolutionary movement, hoisted a Cuban flag from the statue's crown in protest against the brutal regime of dictator Fulgencio Batista.

In 1965, on the sixth anniversary of Fidel Castro's rise to power, nineteen Cuban exiles chained themselves to the balcony of the statue's base. The part of the balcony they chose to chain themselves to is approximately twenty feet below the statue's foot, which stands upon broken shackles, symbolizing the power of liberty to snap the chains of tyranny.

On Cuban Independence Day, in 1966, a Cuban refugee hung their flag from Miss Liberty's pedestal.

In 1967, 1,700 people went to Liberty Island in below-freezing weather to show their support for the federal government's antipoverty programs, whose budgets were threatened.

In 1971 fifteen members of Vietnam Veterans Against the War barricaded themselves inside the statue to protest the continuance of the war. They hung a United States flag upside down, first from the statue's crown and later from her torch. After forty-two hours they left peacefully.

The Attica Brigade, a student organization, had thirty of its members occupy the Statue of Liberty in 1974 to dramatize the "importance of having President Nixon removed from office." Also that year, several hundred members of New Jersey's Gay Activists Alliance

Fig. 43. Book jacket, *How to Become a Virgin*, by Quentin Crisp. *Courtesy Fontana Paperbacks, England.*

Quentin Crisp
How to
Become a
Virgin

a sequel to
The Naked Civil Servant

FONTANA

organized a "Hold Hands Rally" at the statue, forming a human circle around her base as a gesture of solidarity. This event occurred only a few days before the New York City Council's vote against a bill to bar discrimination in employment on the basis of sexual orientation.

In 1977, twenty-nine members of the Committee to Free the Five occupied the Statue of Liberty. They demanded freedom for four (one had died) Puerto Rican nationalists, who had been imprisoned since 1954 for trying to gain Puerto Rican independence by attempting to assassinate congressmen on the floor of the United States Capitol. They stayed inside the statue for eight hours and flew a Puerto Rican flag throughout their vigil.

Six demonstrators chained themselves inside the statue's crown in 1977 to protest the arrest and torture in Iran of eighteen political opponents of Shah Reza Pahlavi. Their banner, hung from Miss Liberty's crown, read, "Free the 18." Five hours later the National Parks Service was able to obtain a court order requiring the protesters to leave.

In 1979, after the shah of Iran had been deposed, seven demonstrators chained themselves to the statue's railing and hung a banner from her crown that demanded the deposed monarch be returned to his homeland and "tried and punished." At the time, the shah was residing in a New York City hospital recuperating from gallbladder surgery. The protesters were arrested for disorderly conduct upon exiting the statue.

The most imaginative form of protest at the Statue of Liberty took place in 1980, when two members of the Committee for the Defense of Geronimo Pratt used suction cups and mountaineering equipment to scale the statue. They did this to protest a California court decision dismissing an appeal by Mr. Pratt. Pratt, a former member of the Black Panthers, convicted of murder in 1972, had at that time served nine of the seven-years-to-life term he was sentenced to. His supporters believed he had been framed by the Federal Bureau of Investigation's Cointelpro—an undercover

Fig. 44. Supertramp, *Breakfast in America.* © 1978 A&M Records, Inc.
Used by permission. All rights reserved.

Fig. 45. American Salute, Arthur Fiedler/Boston Pops. Artist Al Hirschfeld. © 1972 RCA Records.

counterintelligence program that used illegal tactics to disrupt the activities of political organizations.

The climbers stayed aloft overnight and unfurled a banner that read, "Liberty was framed. Free Geronimo Pratt." The National Parks Service issued a statement to the press estimating that the cost of repairing the damage caused by the climbers could approach $80,000. After the climbers came down, experts examined the statue and found no damage at all caused by the climbers, but they did find serious corrosion of the statue's exterior caused by pollution and exposure to the elements for almost a hundred years.

The next demonstration at the statue was organized by employees of the federal government. Members of the Immigration and Naturalization Service demonstrated to "focus attention on the problems created by uncontrolled immigration and the Reagan administration's failure to properly direct the agency and its employees." President Reagan had just proposed a "foreign guest worker program" that the agency viewed as unenforceable. They already were overworked and understaffed and expected the proposed program, if put into effect, to make it impossible for them to do their jobs. The demonstrators from the Immigration and Naturalization Service were seeking to limit legal immigration into the United States to 350,000 people a year. In the preceding year 850,000 people had been allowed to legally immigrate to the United States.

The poor state of the world's environment was the next cause that led activists to unfurl banners from the statue. And considering what pollution has done to the statue over the years, it seems a very appropriate place to make that message known.

Demonstrations will no doubt continue at the statue. They draw much attention and media coverage for the cause of the demonstrators.

★   ★   ★

The Statue of Liberty has been used as the official symbol of many organizations and businesses. In 1918 she appeared on the official insignia of the Seventy-seventh Metropolitan Division of the United States Army. She appeared on the official flag of the 1939 World's Fair. In 1955 the Package Designers Council made her the designated emblem for all American manufacturer displays at foreign trade fairs. She is on the emblem of the New York State Chiropractic Association and the logo of both the Liberty Mutual Life Insurance Company and the Manhattan Life Insurance Company.

In 1950 a university professor of history proposed that the Statue of Liberty be substituted for the bald eagle as the symbol of the United States. He argued that since the bald eagle is a bird of prey, the Statue of Liberty would more closely reflect the ideals of the Founding Fathers of this country because it "stands for peace through freedom rather than peace through subjugation."

Miss Liberty's image has been used to represent every political view from the far left to the extreme right; to show the strivings for equality of various minority groups in this country—women, blacks, Hispanics, and gays; to symbolize both American imperialism and American largesse. She has been portrayed as an environmentalist decrying the pollution of our land and as extremely overweight to reflect American mass consumerism. She has been depicted as an innocent young girl, as a seductress, and as a crass, cigarette-smoking, middle-aged woman. She has been a shill for every imaginable product. All these representations, though often contradictory, are understandable, because she is seen through many peoples' eyes.

Fig. 46. Joel Resnicoff, "I Love New York." © *1980. Courtesy of the artist.*

Chapter 2

ARTWORKS

★   ★   ★   ★   ★

Bartholdi's Statue of Liberty has inspired many artists to create interpretations of it as a symbol of American—good and bad.

The earliest painting included in this book is Florine Stettheimer's *New York City Harbor 1918 (Fig. 1)*. It is a detailed view of the New York City waterfront with a gold-leafed Statue of Liberty rising on her pedestal from the sea much as Botticelli's Venus did on her seashell. The analogy is appropriate because Stettheimer was trying to convey in her painting that Liberty was the supreme deity of this land. The promise of liberty is guaranteed by the military, technological, and economic powers of the country.

Frank Riley's *Joy Stick Skyline, N.Y., (Color Plate 1)* shows the statue in a very different light. He depicts her as the individual who pushes the button that sets all the energy and activity flowing in the New York Harbor. Luis Jimenez views the statue as a seductress *(Color Plate 2)*. He implies that her promises of freedom and justice for all have not always been met.

The Mimi Gross/Red Grooms/Ruckus Manhattan Construction Company version of the Statue of Liberty *(Color Plate 3)* reminds me of the type of person who, loaded down with shopping bags, tromps on your foot in her mad dash to get an empty seat on the subway during rush hour. The papier-mâché and garish colors capture the vitality of everyday life in New York. Their Miss Liberty is a good-natured, fun-loving, no-nonsense type of person. Despite the wide-brimmed hat, I doubt very much that, as rumor had it, this cigar-smoking character was modeled after New York's colorful former congresswoman, Bella Abzug.

Roger Brown believes the statue has a duty to defend liberty and uses her in his painting *Liberty Inviting Artists to Take Part in an Exhibition against International Leftist Terrorism* (IRA/PLO/FALN/Red Brigade/Sandinistas/Bulgarians) to rally other artists *(Color Plate 4)*. Ben Schonzeit *(Fig. 2)* has Liberty appearing with two other American icons—George Washington and a glass of Coca-Cola—as if to say today's product-oriented society is what carries the torch of America's world presence, while Washington and the statue are but fuzzy memories.

Richard Lindner's 1968 painting *Out of Towners* *(Color Plate 9)* is part of his New York City series. Born in Germany, Lindner fled to England during World War II. He worked for years there as an illustrator and continued to make his living by illustration after he immigrated to this country. When he was appointed to the staff of Brooklyn's Pratt Institute, he gave up illustration forever and transferred his narrative abilities to his paintings. Each of his paintings tells a story that is easy to decipher. In *Out of Towners* we have two middle-aged tourists visiting New York City for the first time. Of course they want to see the sights and go to a few Broadway shows and visit some of the city's major cultural institutions. The first thing they plan to do is visit the Statue of Liberty, but they are not really interested in seeing her. If you look closely at the painting, they are not looking at her at all. Their main concern is getting a postcard with a

Fig. 47. Piels poster. *Courtesy the Stroh Brewery Company.*

Fig. 48 (left). Toshiba ad, 1979. *Courtesy Toshiba Corporation.*

Fig. 49 (above). Atarax ad. *Courtesy Pfizer, Inc.*

photograph of the statue so they can send it back home to let everyone know they have visited her, since that's what you are supposed to do when you come to New York. They're actually hurrying by her to get to a restaurant where the woman's cousin ate and saw Dustin Hoffman. Not a very charitable view of tourists, but a candid statement about the human urge to rush through events we feel obligated to take part in so we can get on to doing what we really want to do.

Ludovico de Luigi's *New Liberty of Venice (Fig. 3)* has survived the flooding of that city. How she got there is totally conjecture, but I wouldn't be surprised if she was carried there by the tidal waves that followed the melting of the polar ice caps after the next nuclear war.

Saul Steinberg interprets the Statue of Liberty as a beacon lighting the way for the ship of state *(Color Plate*

5). Steinberg's cartoonlike images have a satirical edge and are geometrically precise. The ship of state has Liberty in the prow, closely followed by two politicians in the guise of baseball players. Is Steinberg suggesting that we Americans naïvely view politics as a game with only two opposing teams? The politicians are followed by Abraham Lincoln, who is raising the flag and providing a perch for the national symbol, the bald eagle. Behind Lincoln towers Peace in the guise of an ornate drum majorette, definitely a more military than peaceful figure. Business is represented in the cap and flowing robes of an academic. He is followed by Order, a man wearing the fez and emblem of a fraternal organization. These last two beings sit lowest in the center of the ship and seem to provide the dull, everyday stability necessary to keep the vessel upright. Behind Order stands Law in the form of a western sheriff or cowboy; a figure of frontier justice, not always the fairest or most reliable. The remaining figure in the ship is an American Indian portraying Freedom. Steinberg might be suggesting a way of life removed from contemporary America with this figure, but I doubt it. Freedom sits in the back of the boat, grudgingly accepted by his shipmates but kept in his place where he can do no harm. Above the ship float the angels of Science and Fiction trumpeting our nation's cultural and technological achievements. The ship itself is named after the famous science-fiction writer Jules Verne. Is the ship on a journey around the world to spread the values of its passengers? Or is it bound for the bottom of the sea? Is Steinberg trying to tell us that America's values are imaginary, and that our true concerns are that of the mermaid? Superficially we are concerned with fun, but underneath everything else lies a desire for profit. Whatever the exact meaning of Steinberg's characters, they are made gentle by the charming idiosyncratic shapes he gives them.

Peter Max, whose electrically colored art seemed to appear in every available space, from dinner plates to the sides of city buses, just a few years ago, has created an

Fig. 50. American Savings Bank poster, 1984.

70

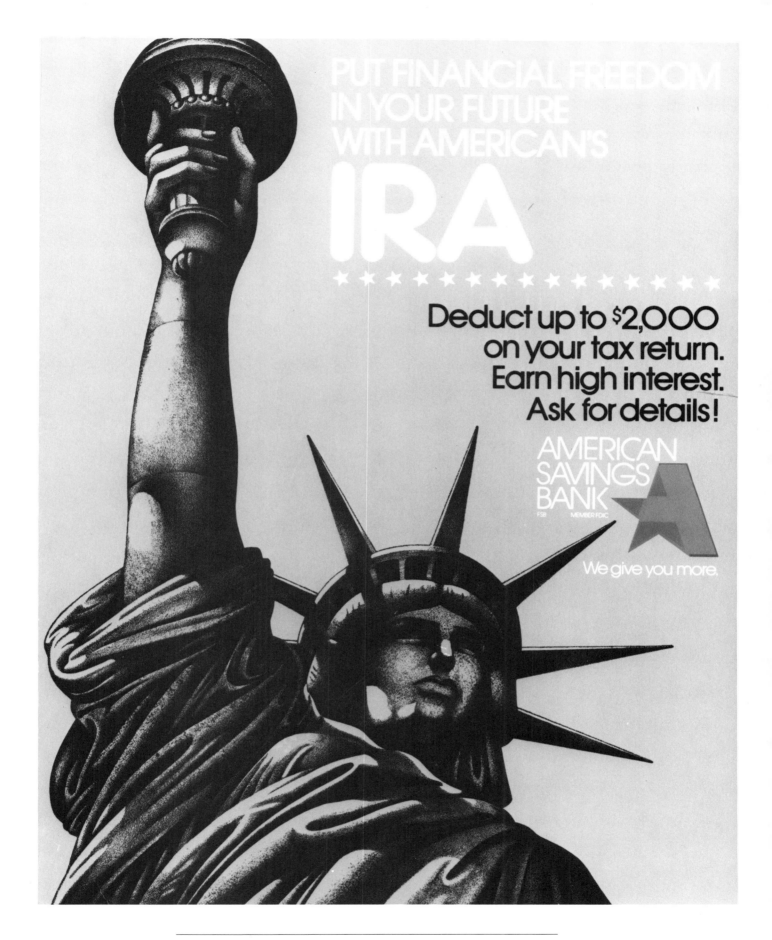

interpretation of the statue that is very beautiful. One of a series of six paintings of the statue that he created on Independence Day, July 4, 1981, is included in this book (Fig. 4). I like to think of it as the Melting Pot Statue of Liberty. From a mixture of many different colors, he's created a unified, coherent form that is strengthened by the diversity of its parts.

Rem Koolhaas and Madelon Vriesendorp's vision of the statue's future, as expressed in their 1975 painting *New Jersey (Fig. 5),* is very peaceful. Liberty Island has become a tropical paradise complete with palm trees and the obligatory beautiful sunset. The statue has gone

Fig. 51 (above). TAP Portuguese Airways ad, 1969. *Courtesy TAP Air Portugal.*

Fig. 52 (right). El Al Airlines ad.

New York to Tel Aviv non-stop
only EL AL does it.

More nonstops to th

More New York nonstops. More
New York wide-bodies. And discount
fares, too. What more could you ask fo

Fig. 53. Eastern Airlines ad, 1984.

We hold America together.

Talon

626 Arch Street, Meadville, PA 16335

topless in this new climate. The Chrysler Building is in ruins and I think the statue is using part of it as her bed.

The Statue of Liberty is an ominous, lurking presence in Ivan Kustura's *Reclining Figure/Post Atomic (Color Plate 6)*. She sadly watches over a horribly malformed human being as if to say, "Too bad—you had your chance in this beautiful world and you destroyed yourselves."

The Haitian artist Ludovic Booz's painting of the statue *(Fig. 6)* idealizes her as a sort of goddess. His Liberty is more concerned with providing for the immediate human needs of food and shelter than with any abstract ideals.

Erté's version of the statue, *Liberty, Fearless and Free (Color Plate 7)*, reaches back to the time of the ancient Greeks and Romans. Clad in a toga, his slim goddess carries high the torch of liberty as she runs through the night heavens, inspiring mortals to live by the heavenly ideals of liberty.

James Morlock's *Liberty (Color Plate 10)* is a beautiful young woman whose major purpose seems to be as an inspiration for fashionable young models. Fashion is a form of freedom of expression that is often overlooked. Liberty by Martinique *(Fig. 7)* has a fashion sense all her own; as an Indian maiden with a cape made of Old Glory, she sends the dove of peace out into the land. Don Hazlitt's sense of the statue is as an abstraction; he represents her in his sculpture *Liberty Stacks (Fig. 8)*, but does not personify her.

The statue has inspired work in various mediums. Laura Wilensky's *July 4th Weekend (Fig. 9)* is made of ceramic. The students of Seth Low Junior High in Brooklyn made a mosaic Statue of Liberty in 1984 *(Color Plate 17c)*. The parents of the students at Friends Seminary made a Melting Pot Quilt in 1983 that included a panel on the statue *(Color Plate 17a)*. In 1982, Rocky Pinciotti made a neon *Liberty (Fig. 10)*. In 1985, Reader Mail, of the *New York Daily News*, made a needlepoint version of the statue *(Color Plate 17b)*. Erik Gronborg has

Fig. 54. Talon ad, 1981. Courtesy Chester Gore Company.

Fig. 55 (above). WAPP ad, 1984.

Fig. 56 (right). Pepsi ad. Courtesy Pepsico, Inc.

THE STATUE OF LIBERTY - ELLIS ISLAND
CENTENNIAL COMMISSION
"Peanuts/Liberty"

Public Service Announcements
Available in :60, :30 Versions
60 SECONDS

Please do not run after November 1, 1985.

(MEDLEY PATRIOTIC
MUSIC ON PIANO)

(MUSIC UNDER)
LINUS: America! We
made it!

SALLY: I'm so happy.
LINUS: Look, the Statue
of Liberty! SALLY: Isn't
she beautiful.

LUCY: I don't feel so good.

C. BROWN: You look
alright to me. Where does
it hurt?

LUCY: All over. I need lots
of fixing.

C. BROWN: That's going
to be expensive. Where are
we going to get the money?

LUCY: You blockhead!
I'm the Statue of Liberty.
If we ask people to help,
they will.

Everyone loves me.

LINUS: She's right. To
fix what ails the Statue
of Liberty, we need lots
of money.

SALLY: So, if you out
there want to help, send
your contributions to:

The Lady. Box 1986,
New York. Or call
1-800-The Lady. LUCY: It
would make me feel a lot
better.

C. BROWN: Say it, gang!

ALL: Keep the torch lit.

C. BROWN: I love her.

Fig. 57 (left). NYNEX ad, 1984. *Courtesy Young & Rubicam.*

Fig. 58 (right). Charles M. Schulz, Peanuts/ Liberty, 1984. *Courtesy Kenyon & Eckhardt and the Ad Council.*

made a porcelain cup of the statue *(Fig. 11)*, and Michel Proulx has photographed a neon sign of her *(Fig. 12)*.

Tomie Arai has stressed the importance of women in his mural *Women Hold Up Half the Sky (Fig. 13)*. Irva Mandelbaum was inspired by the centennial in her piece *Happy Birthday, Liberty (Fig. 14)*. In the late nineteenth century the J. L. Mott Ironworks used the statue as the central figure in a weathervane they manufactured *(Fig. 15)*. Very few were made and they are extremely rare today.

Baldo Diodato's *Italian Lyric (Fig. 16)* captures the romance of liberty. Peter Passuntino envisions liberty as one of the essential characters in American society. She is a concerned onlooker as Christ enters New York City *(Fig. 17)* and is one of the participants in his *American Still Life (Fig. 18)*.

Fig. 59. Oscar Mayer ad, 1984.

Fig. 60 (right). Stroh Brewery Co. poster, 1984.

Dimanche Sunday Sonntag	Lundi Monday Montag	Mardi Tuesday Dienstag	Mercredi Wednesday Mittwoch	Jeudi Thursday Donnerstag	Vendredi Friday Freitag	Samedi Saturday Samstag
		1	2	3	4	5
6	7	8	9	10	11	12
13	14	15	16	17	18	19
20	21	22	23	24	25	26
27	28	29	30	31		

Août August August 1978

genuine spare parts FIAT A

Fig. 61 (this page). FIAT calendar, 1978. *Courtesy Fiat Auto S.p.A., Italy.*

Fig. 62 (right page). Campbell Soup Co. calendar, 1985.

BARSQUALDI'S STATUE
LIBERTY FRIGHTENING THE WORLD.
BEDBUGS ISLAND. N.Y. HARBOR.

Fig. 63. Thomas Worth, Currier & Ives, 1884. *Courtesy Library of Congress.*

Fig. 64. Thomas Nast,
Harper's Weekly, 1881.
Courtesy Library of Congress.

world-renowned artist, but he accepted a $90-a-month position with the Treasury Department as an assistant in the Procurement Division just so he could paint his frescoes there. In a period of seven weeks, Marsh completed his eight large horizontal and eight small vertical paintings that comprised his version of the statue. In the smaller spaces, Marsh painted scenes of the great early explorers of America. In the eight larger spaces, he followed the course of a large ship as it entered New York Harbor: as it took on a pilot, was met by the Coast Guard and boarded by government officials, passed by the Statue of Liberty, served as the place for a press conference with movie star Greta Garbo, and as it was brought to the pier by tugboats and finally unloaded its cargo. The paintings cost the government $1,560 to produce. Today they are valued at almost $1 million. The U.S. Custom House is currently undergoing restoration; when it reopens, it will be as a museum of and monument to the victims of the Holocaust.

The two most popular icons of the pop-art movement, which became prominent in the 1960s, are the Statue of Liberty and Marilyn Monroe. Robert Rauschenberg, one of the most famous pop artists, often used the statue in his work, aptly illustrating his often quoted statement "Painting relates to both art and life. Neither can be made. I try to act in the gap between the two." Blurring the distinction between art and real life, the Statue of Liberty, the epitome of the American dream of prosperity and freedom, stands strong among the beauty and decay of urban America in his painting *Estate (Fig. 26).*

Farwell Perry's untitled painting *(Fig. 27)* is one of the most openly patriotic pieces of artwork included in this book. He simply equates the statue with the flag, and says one could not exist without the other. Cosimo Scianna's *Crying Liberty (Fig. 28)* suggests the statue's sadness for her ideals that have not been realized.

Chapter 3

CELEBRITIES

★　　　★　　　★　　　★　　　★

Three different celebrities are represented here as the Statue of Liberty. The late Golda Meir *(Fig. 29),* former prime minister of Israel, was photographed in 1919 as the statue in a patriotic pageant held in Milwaukee, Wisconsin. The poet André Breton *(Fig. 30)* is featured on the cover of his collection of poems *Cherry Trees Secured Against Hares.* The artwork for Breton's book jacket was done by his good friend the world-famous artist Marcel Duchamp. The third celebrity, Richard Nixon *(Fig. 31),* was depicted as Liberty giving the finger to the GI Bill of Rights. His administration sponsored legislation that greatly reduced and in some cases terminated benefits that had been guaranteed to members of the armed forces since the end of World War II. The drawing of Nixon was done by Edward Sorel.

YOU buy a LIBERTY BOND LEST I PERISH

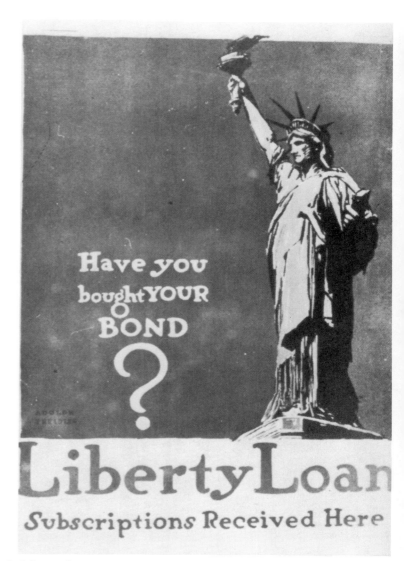

Figs. 65, 66, 67 (left and above). Liberty Loan posters, 1917.
Courtesy Chemical Bank Archives.

Figs. 68, 69 (above left, right). Liberty Loan posters, 1917.
Courtesy Chemical Bank Archives.

Fig. 70 (right). Joseph Pennell, 1917. Courtesy U.S. Dept. of the
Interior/National Park Service.

IOSEPH PENNELL DEL.

THAT LIBERTY SHALL NOT
PERISH FROM THE EARTH
BUY LIBERTY BONDS
FOURTH   LIBERTY   LOAN

Chapter 4

REPLICAS

★　　　★　　　★　　　★　　　★

Replicas of the Statue of Liberty have always been popular collector's items. Bartholdi himself cast 200 miniatures, which were sold to raise funds for the statue's pedestal. He also made a one-sixteenth scale model for the Hanoi Exposition of 1887. Not a very shrewd businessman, he signed away his copyright to the statue and didn't receive any royalties from all the models of it that were later manufactured.

Though the Statue of Liberty was a gift from France to the people of the United States, the American people have so taken her as our own that we have a long tradition of giving replicas of it to other countries as a symbol of America and American goodwill. The first instance of this occurred in 1889 when American residents of Paris donated a thirty-six-foot replica to that city *(Fig. 32)*. It was erected on the Seine under the Grenelle Bridge in view of the Eiffel Tower and can still be seen there today.

In 1917 the *New York Herald,* one of the city's leading daily newspapers during the period 1900 to 1924, sponsored a benefit performance at the New York Hippo-drome to raise funds for a Statue of Liberty to be donated to Russia. It was meant to show America's solidarity with the October Revolution.

New York City was once the proud home of two large replicas of the statue. The first was built in 1902 for a Russian immigrant who set it atop his warehouse at 47 West Sixty-fourth Street, directly across from what is now Lincoln Center. Like the original, it had a staircase leading to its crown. Its torch when lit could be seen for a mile. A storm in 1912 blew the torch off and weakened the staircase. For safety reasons, visitors are no longer allowed to enter the statue, but it can be seen from the street.

In 1944 the Motion Picture War Activities Committee of New York erected in Times Square an asbestos model of Miss Liberty one-third the size of the one on Liberty Island (Fig. 33). Its purpose was to sell Liberty Loan Bonds—one of the ways the federal government financed World War II—and the base of the statue housed a booth where the bonds were sold. On a stage above the booth, performances were given to sell bonds and raise public morale. To inaugurate the bond drive, President Franklin D. Roosevelt, in a live nationwide radio broadcast, pushed a button on his desk at the White House that lit the torch of the Times Square statue. The statue was given to New York City at the end of the war, but in 1946 it had to be dismantled due to an irreparable crack that made the structure a potential hazard.

In 1950 the Boy Scouts of America embarked on a fund-raising drive to enable them to buy 4,000 eight-and-a-half-foot cast-copper replicas of Miss Liberty. They planned to place these statues at courthouses, state capitols, schoolhouses, and other public buildings in each

Fig. 71 (right). Simon S. Kwon, Korean Catholic Apostolate of the Brooklyn Diocesan Migration Office announcement of services at Queens College and St. Patrick's Cathedral, celebrating the bicentennial of Korean Catholicism.

한국천주교회 200주년
미동부지역 경축대회

신앙 **강연회** 및 경축 **미사**

이 땅에 빛을

연사 : 정하권 신부

강연회 (제 1 일)

일시 : 1984년 10월 5일 (금) 오후 8시
장소 : QUEENS COLLEGE 대강당

　　　(제 2 일)

일시 : 1984년 10월 6일 (토) 오후 8시
장소 : ST. PATRICK 대성당

미사일시 : 1984년 10월 7일 (일)
　　　　　　　　　　　　오후 8 시
장소 : ST. PATRICK 대성당

주최 : 미동부지역
　　　　한인천주교회

Fig. 72 (this page). Tomi Ungerer, *Eat*, 1967. *Courtesy of the artist.*

Fig. 73 (right page). Tomi Ungerer, *Kiss for Peace*, 1968. *Courtesy of the artist.*

of the Boy Scout districts of the country. Before they completed their plans, however, the National Sculpture Society condemned the quality of the reproductions as "very inadequate." The fund-raising drive was halted, but many of the replicas had already been put on display (see for example, *Figs. 34, 35, and 36*) and can still be viewed today. They have a charm of their own, and the towns and cities that have them on display are justly proud of them.

One of the first seventy replicas produced for the Boy Scouts was given to the Boy Scouts of the Philippines—it was erected in Manila. And in 1952 Japan received one of the Boy Scout replicas as a gift from the Custom Brokers and Forwarders Association of America. Its final destination was the newly constructed Peace

Fig. 74 (this page). Poster, *March for Religious Freedom*, New York Committee for Religious Freedom.

Fig. 75 (right page). Twenty-seventh Biennial Clergy-Laity Conference of the Greek Orthodox Archdiocese of North and South America.

ΕΛΛΗΝΙΚΗ ΟΡΘΟΔΟΞΟΣ ΑΡΧΙΕΠΙΣΚΟΠΗ ΒΟΡΕΙΟΥ Κ' ΝΟΤΙΟΥ ΑΜΕΡΙΚΗΣ

-GREEK ORTHODOX ARCHDIOCESE OF NORTH AND SOUTH AMERICA-

TWENTY SEVENTH BIENNIAL CLERGY-LAITY CONGRESS

ΕΙΚΟΣΤΗ ΕΒΔΟΜΗ ΚΛΗΡΙΚΟΛΑΙΚΗ ΣΥΝΕΛΕΥΣΙΣ

"We look for new
heavens and a new earth,
wherein dwelleth
righteousness"
(II Peter 3:13)

«Καινούς δέ Ουρανούς
καί Γῆν καινήν
προσδοκῶμεν ἐν οἷς
δικαιοσύνη κατοικεῖ»
(2 Πέτρ. 3:13)

27th BIENNIAL CLERGY-LAITY CONGRESS/JULY 1-5, 1984/NEW YORK

Fig. 76. American Is Beautiful, 1983. *Courtesy A.F.L.-C.I.O.*

Center in Nagasaki. The city of Hiroshima had announced in 1947 plans to erect a copy of the Statue of Liberty on the site of a feudal castle destroyed by the first atomic bomb used during World War II. It was planned "to show the dedication of this atom-blasted city to world peace."

In 1952 a former United States ambassador to the Philippines launched a drive to raise $500,000 for the building of a copy of the Statue of Liberty on the island of Corregidor, the site of a decisive military victory for the United States during World War II.

In 1958 a thirty-one-foot copy of Miss Liberty was erected on the roof of the home offices of Liberty National Life Insurance Company in Birmingham, Alabama *(Fig. 37)*. The company had been using an image of the statue in their advertising for thirty years prior to erecting their own version.

To fulfill a campaign pledge "to bring the Statue of Liberty to Wisconsin," the Pail and Shovel party, a student group at the University of Wisconsin, erected a version of her in the winter of 1978 and again in 1979 on frozen Lake Mendota. The Statue of Liberty was most recently erected as a large float in the Macy's 1984 Thanksgiving Day Parade.

Chapter 5

COVER
ILLUSTRATIONS

★　　　★　　　★　　　★　　　★

Bartholdi's Statue of Liberty is a real cover girl, having appeared on the covers of more magazines, books, comic books, record albums, and theater programs than any other personality.

The artist Bruce Handy has the statue appearing on the cover of the *Stanford Chaparral* in a pose reminiscent of Marilyn Monroe's famous scene in the movie *The Seven Year Itch*. The statue's skirts have been lifted high into the sky affording us a first-time view of her well-shaped legs *(Color Plate 11)*.

When the Theatre de Poche, in Brussels, presented the play *Macbird*—the *Macbeth* story with the central characters of the Kennedy and Johnson administrations substituted for the original players—they showed the statue on the cover of their theater program as a predatory bird *(Fig. 38)*.

The statue appears regularly on the covers of comic books. Spider-Man, Daredevil, and Captain America have all made daring rescues at the statue *(see Color Plates 18 and 19)*.

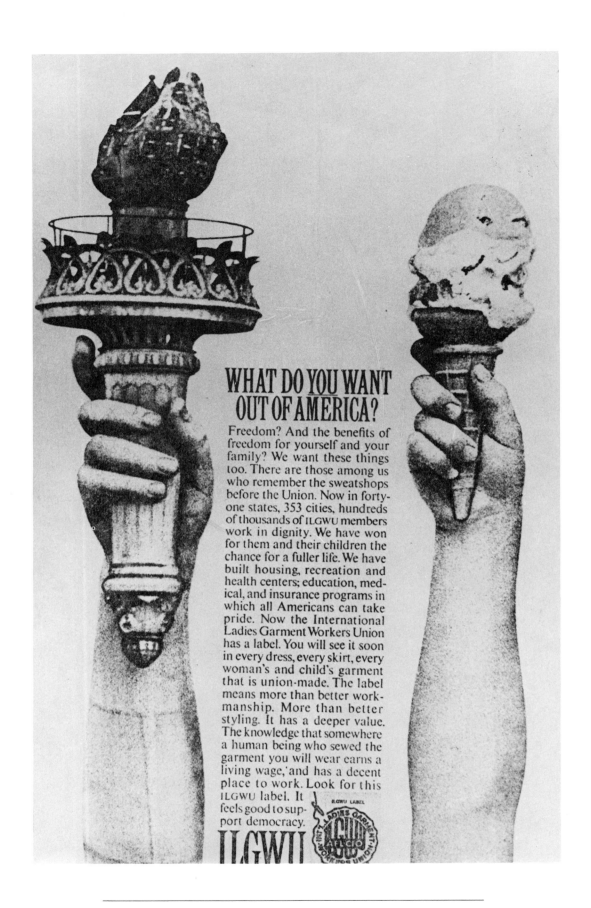

WHAT DO YOU WANT OUT OF AMERICA?

Freedom? And the benefits of freedom for yourself and your family? We want these things too. There are those among us who remember the sweatshops before the Union. Now in forty-one states, 353 cities, hundreds of thousands of ILGWU members work in dignity. We have won for them and their children the chance for a fuller life. We have built housing, recreation and health centers; education, medical, and insurance programs in which all Americans can take pride. Now the International Ladies Garment Workers Union has a label. You will see it soon in every dress, every skirt, every woman's and child's garment that is union-made. The label means more than better workmanship. More than better styling. It has a deeper value. The knowledge that somewhere a human being who sewed the garment you will wear earns a living wage, and has a decent place to work. Look for this ILGWU label. It feels good to support democracy.

ILGWU

Celebrate

WOMEN'S EQUALITY DAY

Around the Clock Watch for the
Equal Rights Amendment
Saturday, August 22, 1981
5th Avenue at 59th Street
Noon to Midnight Saturday August 22nd

Celebrities, entertainment, ERA readings, music, commentary, feminist readings
New York Chapter
National Organization for Women
84 FIFTH AVE., RM. 907, N.Y.C. 10011   (212) 989-7230

Join

Elizabeth Alston: **Redbook** ■ Frank Barbaro: **Democratic and New Alliance Mayoral Candidate** ■ Rosalind Block and the Empire ■ Myrna Blyth: **Ladies Home Journal** ■ Rosemary Brey: **Essence** ■ Mary Burke-Nicholas: **NYS Women's Division Butchers Union** ■ Dr. Narvella Colby: **(Executive Director) Girl Scouts** ■ Alice Cordona: **Hispanic Women's Center, HACER** ■ Paulina Cortes: **Asian-Pacific Women's Political Caucus** ■ Nan Cox: **Church Women United** ■ Carmen Cruz: **Image — Women's Action Committee** ■ Miriam Friedlander: **Councilwoman** ■ Denise Fuge: **National Organization for Women** ■ Patia Gaugh: **railroad worker** ■ Elaïne Gleason: **Communication Workers of America** ■ Rosemary Goldford: **Women in Apprenticeship** ■ **Women Office Workers** ■ Elizabeth Janeway: **feminist philosopher** ■ Jane Kelly: **Women in the Trades** ■ Dorchen Leidholdt: **Women Against Pornography** ■ Margaret Lewin, M.D.: **American Medical Women's Association** ■ Ruth Messinger: **Councilwoman** ■ **Mobilization for Survival** ■ Delores Moss: **United Methodist Church** ■ Janet O'Hare: **NY Women Against Rape** ■ Lenore Parker: **Young Women's Christian Association** ■ **Safety and Fitness Exchange** ■ **NY Civil Liberties Union** ■ Lynn Hecht Schafran: **Commission on the Status of Women** ■ Sandra Schnur: **Women with Disabilities United** ■ Sadie Smalls: **Nurses for Political Action** ■ Peggy Smith: **Women's Section, National Black United Front** ■ Ann Sparks: **St. Vincent's Rape Crisis** ■ Susan Wald: **Socialist Workers Party** ■ Emagene Walker: **Coalition of Labor Union Women** ■ Laurie Woods: **National Center on Women and Family Law** ■ and many, many more

Fig. 77 (left page). What Do You Want Out of America?, 1959. Courtesy I.L.G.W.U.

Fig. 78 (this page). Celebrate Women's Equality Day, 1981. Courtesy National Organization for Women.

Fig. 79. *Fight for Women's Liberation*, 1970. *Courtesy Socialist Workers party.*

Plate 17a. Melting Pot Quilt, 1983
Courtesy Friends Seminary, N.Y.

Plate 17b. Needlepoint Statue of Liberty
Courtesy Reader Mail, New York Daily News

Plate 17c. Mosaic Statue of Liberty
Courtesy Seth Lowe Jr. High, Brooklyn, N.Y.

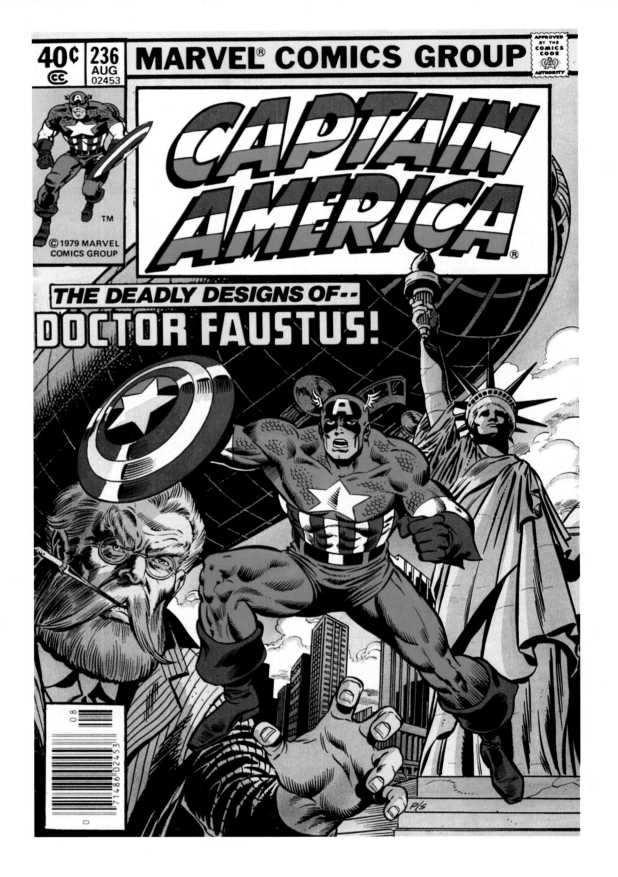

Plate 18.   Captain America #236 (Aug.)

©*1979 Marvel Comics Group*

Plate 21. Alberto Blanco, *World Solidarity with Puerto Rico*

Courtesy OSPAAAL/Cuba

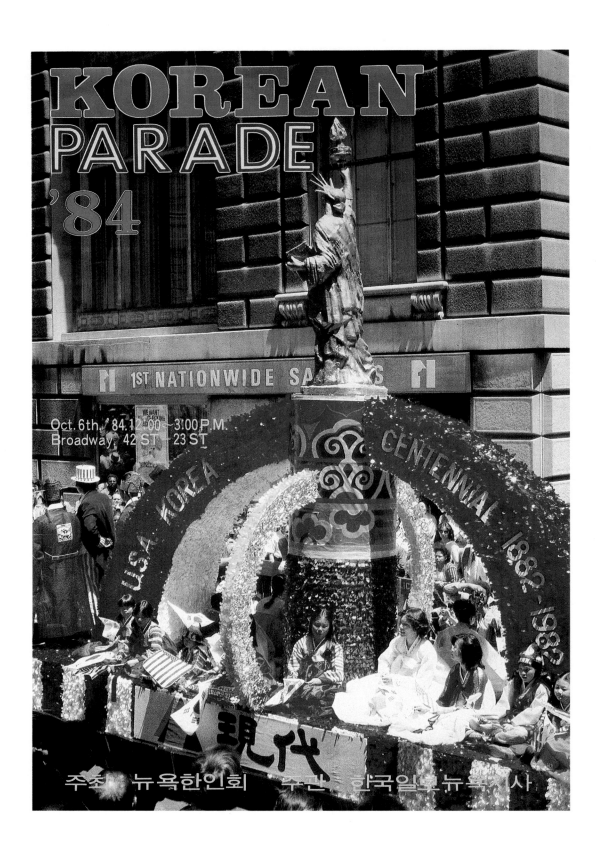

Plate 22. Korean Parade, 1984

Courtesy Korean News

Plate 23. Solidarity Sunday for Soviet Jewry, 1979

Courtesy the Greater New York Conference on Soviet Jewry

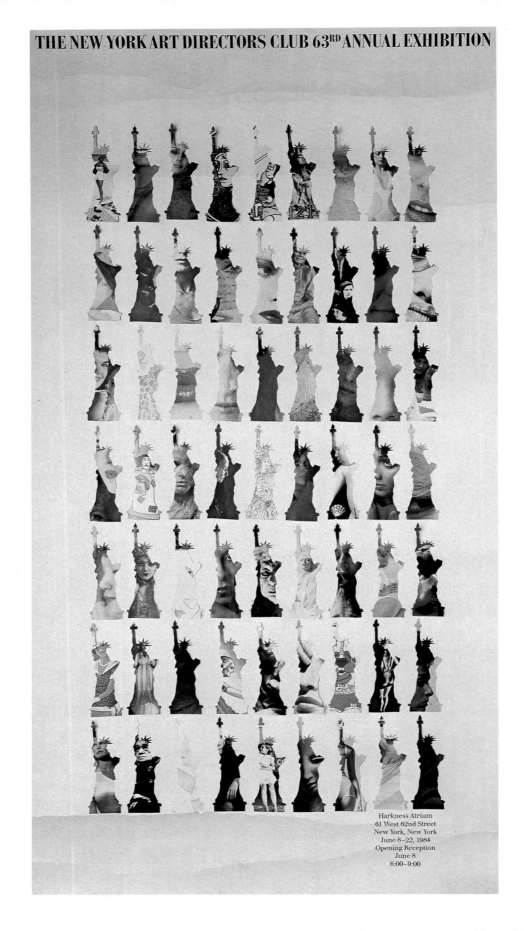

Harkness Atrium
61 West 62nd Street
New York, New York
June 8–22, 1984
Opening Reception
June 8
6:00–9:00

Plate 24. The New York Art Directors Club 63rd Annual Exhibition, Designer Chris Hill

Courtesy New York Art Directors Club

Millimeter magazine emphasized that New York is still a center of television and movie production by placing the statue on its cover *(Fig. 39). The WPA Guide to New York City* has a very stylized art-deco representation of the statue on its cover *(Fig. 40).*

Mad magazine represented the statue's recent reconstruction in their usual zany way. The cover of *Mad (Fig. 41)* has a helicopter holding aloft a giant Q-Tip that is about to enter and clean the statue's ear.

Arabia: The Islamic World Review has portrayed the statue as a pistol-packing mama pointing her gun at the equally armed Russians, with the Arabs caught in the middle of the conflict *(Fig. 42).*

Quentin Crisp, appearing along with the statue on the cover of his book *How to Become a Virgin (Fig. 43),* visually suggests that Miss Liberty is the oldest virgin around. The magazine *Vanity Fair* depicted the statue on their cover much in their own image with an elegant model clothed in the U.S. flag *(Color Plate 12).*

On the Supertramp album *Breakfast in America (Fig. 44),* the Statue of Liberty is represented by a deliriously happy waitress with a menu in her left hand and a glass of milk held high in her right. Arthur Fiedler is the subject of a Hirschfeld caricature that depicts him as the statue on the cover of his *American Salute* album *(Fig. 45).*

The statue has recently become a popular image on postcards. "Mr. Liberty" by Michael Rock *(Color Plate 13)* is a gay clone of the statue, and Joel Resnicoff's "I Love New York" postcard *(Fig. 46)* presents Miss Liberty as a shopping-bag lady.

Chapter 6

ADVERTISING

★　　　★　　　★　　　★　　　★

The Statue of Liberty has been used to advertise a wide variety of products, and even the earliest ads took liberties with her image. They used gentle humor to relate their product to the statue, and it was common practice to substitute the product being advertised for the statue's torch or base. Held aloft in the statue's right hand, the product seemed to have the endorsement of Miss Liberty herself, as shown in the four turn-of-the-century ads from the Chemical Bank Archives *(Color Plate 15)*.

Today's advertisers have continued this practice but have refined it. Now advertisers use the statue to say something specific about their product. A 1983 Piels ad *(Fig. 47)* has the statue holding a can of Piels raised high in celebration of both the Brooklyn Bridge's and Piels's one-hundredth anniversary. The ad relates the beer to the monumental architectural and aesthetic achievements of the building of both the Brooklyn Bridge and the Statue of Liberty. The ad implies that since Piels has existed as long as the bridge and longer than the statue,

Fig. 80. Make America a Better Place, Peace Corps, 1968. *Courtesy Young & Rubicam.*

Fig. 81. It Can't Happen Here, 1963. Courtesy American Civil Liberties Union.

"ETERNAL
VIGILANCE
IS THE
PRICE OF
LIBERTY."

Thomas Jefferson

132 West 43rd Street, New York, New York 10036

Fig. 82. Eternal Vigilance
Is the Price of Liberty.
Photo Lawrence Frank,
design S. Neil Fujita.
© 1984 A.C.L.U.

Free your mind.   Use your library.

Fig. 83. Free Your Mind. Use Your Library. Artist Bob Weber. *Courtesy American Library Association.*

the beer is of the same quality as these two national historical monuments.

Wise advertisers have learned to use the statue's inherent symbolism as a way to describe and sell their products. A Toshiba ad *(Fig. 48)* shows the statue holding aloft a television remote-control unit. The fact that we associate the statue with freedom has been cleverly used to show us a different type of freedom—the freedom from having to get up and go over to the television every time we want to change the channel. An ad for Atarax *(Fig. 49)* also plays upon our association of freedom with the statue. She is trying to scratch a spot on her back that is just beyond her reach. Atarax is promising her and us "freedom from itch." An ad for the American Savings Bank *(Fig. 50)* talks about economic freedom, and strongly suggests where "It's Worth Saving For." The American Savings Bank, of course.

Airlines often use the Statue of Liberty as a symbol for America in their ad campaigns. See for example the TAP Portuguese Airways, Eastern Airlines, and El Al ads that appear in this book *(Figs. 51, 52, 53)*. I think the most effective of this group is the El Al ad, which visually juxtaposes the statue's torch and crown with a menorah. With very few words they've gotten their message across and gone beyond that to point out a physical and spiritual link between the two lands.

My favorite of all the ads reproduced in this book is the one for Talon zippers *(Fig. 54)*. It perfectly integrates the symbolism of the statue with the idea the company is trying to get across about their product. We're given a view of the statue's back with a Talon zipper running the length of her spine and the words "We hold America together."

There are ads that use the statue to personify New York City. A WNBC Radio 66 ad *(Color Plate 20)* does this. The statue is the dominant image, towering center stage above the statue of Prometheus in Rockefeller Center and flanked by the Brooklyn Bridge, the Chrysler Building, the World Trade Center's Twin Tow-

Fig. 84. *Immigration Museum Statue of Liberty*, Design Ivan
Chermayeff, Chermayeff & Geismar Associates.

ers, and Radio City Music Hall. A WAPP radio ad *(Fig. 55)* also uses the statue to personify New York City. She wears sunglasses and a WAPP T-shirt, implying that she and all of New York "Rock with WAPP."

There are even ads that use the statue to imply that use of their product ensures the continuance of the America symbolized by the statue. A World War II Pepsi-Cola ad *(Fig. 56)* says openly, "Defend Our Liberty—Drink Pepsi Cola," and a 1983 ad for NYNEX *(Fig. 57)* warns, "Without us, the home of free speech could lose the power of speech."

The fund-raising campaign for the statue's restoration has generated many ads. The characters from Charles M. Schulz's comic strip "Peanuts" have been enlisted to do their part in raising the necessary funds *(Fig. 58)*. Many corporations have made sizable donations to the restoration fund in exchange for being designated official sponsors and the right to carry the official logo of the U.S. Statue of Liberty Ellis Island Bicentennial Commission on their advertising. The Oscar Mayer ad *(Fig. 59)* reproduced here is from one of the numerous official sponsors. Corporations have found innovative ways to raise the money they donated to the restoration fund. The Stroh Brewery sponsored a "Run for Liberty" *(Fig. 60)*.

Ads for foreign countries have often used the statue to represent the United States—for example the ad for *Time* magazine in France *(Color Plate 14)* and the FIAT calendar in Italy *(Fig. 61)*. Familiar corporate trademarks are being made to resemble the statue and then used in the company's advertising. The Campbell Kids who appear on the cover of Campbell's 1985 calendar *(Fig. 62)* are a perfect example of this.

The statue will continue to be used in ads as long as there is an America that aspires to her ideals. The business of America is business, and the statue is as much a part of the commercial interests in this country as she is its physical symbol.

Fig. 85. Women and the Arts, 1978. Design Seymour Chwast. Courtesy Pushpin Lubalin Peckolick.

Chapter 7

POSTER ART

★　　　★　　　★　　　★　　　★

The Statue of Liberty has political, religious, social, and economic meanings. Her great significance as a symbol has led the widest range of groups imaginable to use her as a means of advancing their own causes or beliefs.

One of the earliest political artworks that used the statue appeared in this country in 1886. It was a racist print manufactured by Currier and Ives *(Fig. 63).* Entitled *Barsqualdi's Liberty Frightening the World,* it showed a heavy black woman carrying a book of port charges for New York Harbor. It was feared at the time that the proposed port charges would divert shipping from the city in favor of less expensive ports.

Representing Liberty as death was Thomas Nast's way of suggesting that the project to raise the statue on Bedloe's Island was dead due to the seeming impossibility of raising adequate funds. In 1881 when this illustration *(Fig. 64)* appeared in *Harper's Weekly,* the outlook for the statue was very grim.

Fig. 86. Movie poster, *The Return of Captain Invincible.* Courtesy Seven Key Films, Australia.

During World War I the statue appeared in many posters that urged the public to buy Liberty Bonds *(Figs. 65–70)*. One of these posters, "That Liberty Shall Not Perish from the Earth," by Joseph Pennell, became the most popular poster of its time. In fact Pennell later wrote a best-selling book about it.

The 1984 "Korean Parade" poster *(Color Plate 22)* marks the centennial of Korean immigration to the

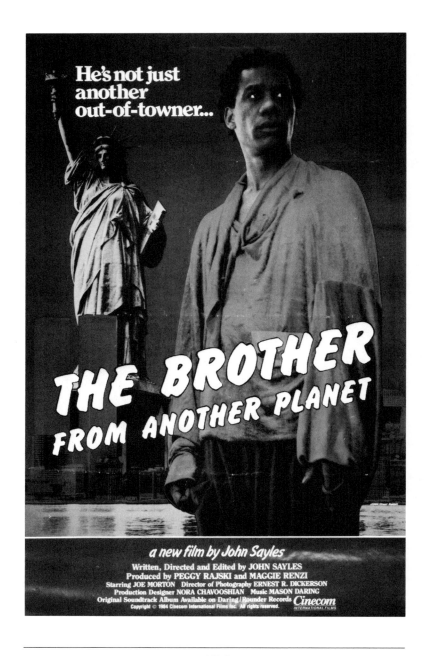

United States. The poster of the statue holding high the flag of Puerto Rico *(Color Plate 21)* was made by a Cuban artist and calls for world solidarity with the Puerto Rican people and their efforts to become a sovereign nation independent of the United States.

Tomi Ungerer's statue posters were made during the Vietnam War. One shows Liberty being shoved down the throat of an Oriental *(Fig. 72);* the other depicts a Vietnamese being forced to kiss Liberty's ass *(Fig. 73)*— two images that powerfully illustrate the unconscionable acts sometimes cloaked in the name of Liberty.

Freedom of religion has long been synonymous with the United States, and the Statue of Liberty has always been an icon of this freedom, whether it be the ecumenical ideal of religious freedom as epitomized by the poster for the March for Religious Freedom *(Fig. 74)*

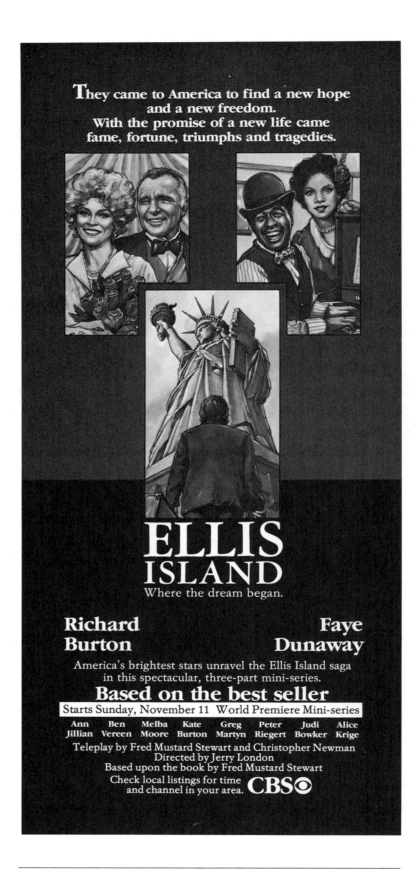

Fig. 89. Ellis Island TV
miniseries. © *1985, CBS.*

Fig. 90. Democracy in America, Tim Miller, NEXT WAVE, Brooklyn Academy of Music. Design Harold Miller. © *Mike Glier 1984.*

or more specifically of oppressed religious minorities as shown in the "Solidarity Sunday" poster *(Color Plate 23)* and the poster that memorializes the Korean Catholics martyred for their faith *(Fig. 71),* or just the simple freedom to gather and worship as expressed by the poster of the Greek Orthodox Archdiocese *(Fig. 75).*

The labor movement, which has done so much to shape America into the country it is today, has used

Fig. 91. *Gotta Get Away*, Radio City Music Hall, New York City.
Artist Don Dailey. *Courtesy Lavaty Studio.*

the statue in two memorable posters: one urging patriotic Americans to buy American, union-made products *(Fig. 76)*; the other pointing up the achievements of the American labor movement in providing a decent standard of living for all Americans *(Fig. 77)*.

As the most recognizable female symbol of this country, Miss Liberty has been particularly useful to the women's liberation movement in its struggle for female equality. The New York Chapter of NOW used the statue in its poster for Women's Equality Day *(Fig. 78)*, and the Socialist Workers party raised the issue in a campaign poster featuring the statue with a raised right fist inside the symbol for female *(Fig. 79)*.

A Peace Corps poster urged Americans to make this country a better place by going to other countries to lend a helping hand *(Fig. 80)*. The American Civil Liberties Union warned us of threats to our democratic rights by putting a moustache on the statue and making her resemble Adolf Hitler, reminding us it *can* happen here *(Fig. 81)*. They also used the statue in a poster recalling Thomas Jefferson's admonition that "eternal vigilance is the price of liberty" *(Fig. 82)*. An American Library Association poster saying "Free your mind. Use your library" *(Fig. 83)* also echoes Jefferson's view of democracy by calling for the public to become well informed.

Fred Marcellino has transplanted the statue to Washington *(Color Plate 16)*. Her presence hovers over the country's center of political power, a reminder to the government of its responsibility to its citizens.

The Immigration Museum has appropriately chosen the statue to represent it on its poster *(Fig. 84)*, while the New York Art Directors Club has used the basic outline of the statue to represent many images used in commercial illustration *(Color Plate 24)*. Seymour Chwast's version of the statue *(Fig. 85)* recalls the art-deco style. Since his poster is for a conference on women in the arts, the statue's tablet has been replaced with an artist's palette and brushes.

Chapter 8

ENTERTAINMENT

★ ★ ★ ★ ★

The Statue of Liberty has appeared in movies, plays, and television specials. The only form of popular entertainment that she has not yet appeared in is a rock video, but that will probably happen any day now.

She has made many cameo appearances in movies. Barbra Streisand sailed by her in *Funny Girl.* Alan Arkin flew by her when he played Captain Invincible (see *Fig. 86).* He even maintained a secret hideout in her crown. Daryl Hannah, as the mermaid in the movie *Splash,* started her search for Tom Hanks at the statue. In John Sayles's film *The Brother from Another Planet,* the statue is where Joe Morton, as the alien in search of sanctuary, first arrives *(Fig. 87).*

The statue's most memorable film role was in the science-fiction classic *Planet of the Apes.* Appearing at the end of the film *(Fig. 88),* it was her presence that revealed to the audience that this world controlled by apes was not some distant planet but Earth itself in the distant future.

Bartholdi's Liberty was the inspiration for a 1949 Broadway musical. *Miss Liberty,* written by Robert Sherwood, was about the adventures of a young French girl brought to this country by a newspaper publisher who mistakenly identified her as the original model for the statue and brought her to help boost his paper's circulation. The music for the show was composed by Irving Berlin. The show was choreographed by Jerome Robbins.

The statue is no stranger to television. She is often used in the montages that begin and end the local news shows in New York City, and in 1984 she was featured in the CBS television miniseries *Ellis Island (Fig. 89).*

Tim Miller's *Democracy in America* poster has the statue holding a microphone aloft *(Fig. 90).* He is saying that the voice of liberty is the voice of democracy. The statue is one of the places visited by Liliane Montevecchi in her Radio City musical *Gotta Get Away (Fig. 91),* and is the first thing viewed by Alice, the main character in the 1985 film *Dream Child (Fig. 92).* In the musical review *What's a Nice Country Like You Doing in a State Like This?* the statue is presented as being pregnant *(Fig. 93).* The 1980 film poster for the movie *Escape from New York* has the statue's head lying among the rubble of a violent decaying city *(Fig. 94).*

The old gal's a media star. With her new face-lift and complete body job, she should be even more appealing to the cameras.

Fig. 92. Movie poster, *Dream Child.* ©1985. *Courtesy Thorn EMI.*

music by **Cary Hoffman**   lyrics by **Ira Gasman**

based on an original concept by Ira Gasman, Cary Hoffman and Bernie Travis

with

Betty Lynn Buckley   Sam Freed   Bill La Vallee
Priscilla López   Barry Michlin

musical direction Arnold Gross

directed and choreographed by Miriam Fond

Budd Friedman presents

WHAT'S A NICE COUNTRY LIKE YOU DOING IN A STATE LIKE THIS?

JOE BUDNE

A Red, White & Blue Revue!

Performances Mon.-Sat. evenings.

UPSTAGE at Jimmy's

33 West 52nd St., N.Y. (212) 757-8484

Fig. 93. Musical-revue poster, *What's a Nice Country Like You Doing in a State Like This?* Art Joe Budne. *Courtesy of the artist.*

Fig. 94. Movie poster, *Escape from New York.* © 1980, *Avco Embassy Pictures.*